S0-ADV-726

Sarada Ramakrishna Vivekananda
Associations of Oregon, San Francisco,
New England & Hawaii

Sri

Sarada

Vijnanagita

Her teachings, selected and arranged in verse form
by Babaji Bob Kindler

Published by SRV Associations of Oregon, San Francisco, Hawaii
and New England.

The publication of this book was made possible in part by
The Adelaide and Alexander Hixon Foundation
and other donations from friends and students of
the independent SRV Associations.

For further information write to:
SRV Oregon
P.O. Box 14012
Portland, OR., 97293 USA
or
SRV Hawaii
P.O. Box 380
Paauilo, HI., 96776 USA

Printed in the United States of America

ISBN 1-891893-06-8

Table Of Contents

SRI SARADA DEVI

The Holy Mother

Introduction

The Sri Sarada Vijnanagita is a work undertaken from the impetus of spontaneous inspiration. It was never planned, but came unheralded. While in the midst of working on several other books, the urge suddenly visited and the entire manuscript was compiled within ten days and ten nights.

Those wondrous days and nights were a joy, for the presence of Holy Mother was tangible in a way previously unimaginable. Spiritual moods attended quite frequently during this sublime period, especially in the late evening and early morning hours. Besides Her own will and intent, this can only be attributed to thirty years of meditation on Her blessed form and presence and the many years of japa using the mantra transmitted in sacred ceremony by Her direct disciple and my provisional guru, Swami Aseshananda.

This work proceeded through a gathering of much of what the Holy Mother communicated to Her spiritual children over Her lifetime, gleaned from the growing number of source books that the devotees of the Ramakrishna movement now have available. *Holy Mother* by Swami Nikhilananda, *The Mother As I Saw Her* by Swami Saradeshwarananda, *Holy Mother Sri Sarada Devi* by Swami Gambhirananda, *Sri Sarada Devi the Holy Mother* by Swami Tapasyananda, and compilations like *Sri Sarada Devi the Great Wonder* and *The Gospel of Holy Mother* — these books provided a more than adequate store of pertinent information from which to draw Her auspicious words. A substantial amount of time was thus spent extracting Her statements and teachings from these works and placing them onto computer files into the categories which they suggested.

The result was a huge store of spiritual wealth which subsequently had to be condensed and edited. The intent was to render Her definitive teachings into running verse form so as to provide Her devotees and those wishing to know more about Her with a transmission of Her direct words, free of historical context and the many incidents of Her life so completely rendered in the previously mentioned books.

What emerged as the verses were constructed was exactly that — a transmission of Her teachings and advice on all levels of existence. Throughout, She always emphasizes what is spiritual in nature with a view towards helping striving beings transform limited human nature and transcend the world of Maya. Since She is the beloved consort of Sri Ramakrishna and the precious Mother of all Her children as well, I was careful to insert not only statements having to do with spiritual matters, but also phrases of affection that She often used towards us. Therefore, endearing sayings such as "my dear," "please come," and others are interspersed throughout the text, infusing the intense and profound teachings with a palpable sense of Her grace and tender affection.

The Sri Sarada Vijnanagita provides nothing particularly new, then, its words being recorded earlier. Its uniqueness lies in the fact that it conveys a steady stream of Her wisdom, unimpeded by linear and sequential daily occurrences and free of the meetings and incidents of Her everyday life. Whereas the few collections of small extractions of Her sayings that are available to us are informative and useful as individual teachings and daily remembrances, reading the Sri Sarada Vijnanagita from cover to cover conveys to us some degree of Her enlightenment, demonstrating how vast is Her realization. It informs us as well that this sublime state called realization, often talked about but seldom attained, consists of more than just lofty knowledge and razor-sharp insight, which by itself would be enough to illumine the mind. True compassion devoid of sentimentality, unflagging and selfless service, pure and unwavering devotion to God with form and beyond form, and uncompromising dedication and adherence to Truth must also be included therein. In addition, Her disarming practicality comes forth and amazes us as well, especially in the face of who She truly is.

In my opinion, the real value of Her teachings, set here in poetic verse, lie in noncompromise. Many are the teachers nowadays who attempt to set us aright with the world, conditioning both our minds and their teachings to facilitate an easy complacency which gradually but definitely undermines true and authentic spiritual discipline and realization. But we cannot worship both God and mammon, as Jesus put it, not if we wish to be truly free. In Holy Mother's teachings we do not hear the message of the materialist, the dualist, the worldly-wise or those who hopefully cry "I'm alright, you're alright" and advise us to "be happy," and "follow your bliss." Rather, and to quote Her, we hear *"My children, may you never have to come back to this world again"* and, *"Birth and death are very painful. May you not suffer from them anymore"* and, *"This world is a great mire. Even Brahma and Vishnu gasp in it, what to speak of mankind."* For those who want liberation and pure love for God, then, She is the eternal Light which illumines the well-chosen and well-defined path to Reality and the perfect exemplar of that precious way as well. As one stotram to Her declares, *"Oh Holy Mother, You are mother, wife, nun, teacher, saint and goddess all in one."*

Even taking just one of the above mentioned facets, a preceptor of this stature and quality is obviously not an ordinary guru. She is Paramaguru — the Supreme Preceptor, and Jagadguru, — the teacher of the world. Moreover, She is Jagadjanani, the Mother of the Universe in human form, a fact attested to by the illumined ones who lived around Her, Her spiritual children and by Sri Ramakrishna Himself. Though it was extremely difficult to get such an admission out of Her while She was living, on several isolated occasions She let it slip. I have included a few of these exclamations in this work, declarations such as *"Where will you find another like me? See if you can find my peer"* and, *"People call me Goddess and I too am led to think so. How else can you explain all the strange things that have happened in my life?"* Then, there was Sri Ramakrishna's statement to Her that *"Whoever takes refuge in You, I shall take them by the hand in the last moments and lead them along the path."* Finally, and my favorite, is Her own affirmation of who She is. Once, in reference to being told that she often appeared like an ordinary women under the influence of Maya, She responded: *"Some having seen me involved in activities of the world, have said that I am entangled in Maya. But what to do, for I myself am Mahamaya."*

Throughout this work, it is interesting and revealing to notice the emphasis She placed upon certain beneficial and detrimental areas of life and spiritual practice. Though much of what She said herein was necessarily edited in order to accommodate a small gita of this size, the essentials were retained. In these pages, among purely positive principles, She speaks most predominantly on the importance of dedication to Sri Ramakrishna, on God's boundless grace, and on Herself. Concerning spiritual disciplines She stresses japa and meditation, working on the mind, austerities, and service with compassion. About detrimental tendencies, dangers, limitations and inhibitions to spiritual realization She points out worldliness, karma, and the problem of fault-finding but in particular Her insights on desire and its effects are both beneficially sobering and edifying. Other helpful topics are also raised and treated with adept discourse.

All of the pictures ever taken of Holy Mother in Her lifetime that I am aware of, a total of 32, are lovingly placed throughout the pages of this book, gracing it further. On the cover we have used a copy of the imprint of Her own feet, the original being accomplished with great foresight while She was still embodied.

May Her Feet of pure love, pure knowledge, pure devotion and absolute freedom become our priceless treasure. As Swami Vivekananda so wonderfully puts it: *"Oh! May the Mother of the Universe bestow Her boon of blessing on me, Her child, forevermore. . . ." "Mother Supreme! Oh, May Thy gracious face never be turned away from me, Thy child. . . ." "May She, the primal guide, my shelter be."*

Dedication

To Her precious spiritual children who love Her
first and foremost
and
to the infinite ocean of human beings who reflect
Her Consciousness.

Peace, Peace, Peace.

Holy Mother's birthday,
December 29th, 1999,
ushering in the new millennium

Mother Herself

"I myself am Mahamaya."

My child, you have arrived!
Come! I am overjoyed to see you.
There is a pillow there, bring it and lie down near me.

I am glad to see you, my child.
You must be hungry — here, take some prasad.
Now rest and listen to this song:

My child, I bless you from the bottom of my heart
that you live long, attain devotion, and enjoy peace.
Peace is the principle thing — one needs peace alone.

My dear, if you can get perfect knowledge through my blessings
then I bless you with all my heart and soul.
Is it ever possible for a man to free himself unaided
from the clutches of Maya?
It was for this that the Master performed austerities
to the utmost extent
and gave the results thereof for the redemption of mankind.

Well, this is the Master's kingdom!
No rules and regulations are valid here.
Here the door is open to all.
Whenever one gets the opportunity, one may call on me.

I do not remember having committed any sin since my birth.
I touched the Master at the age of five.
I might not have understood Him at the time,
but He undoubtedly touched me.

Many people now come to me and confide their worries.
They say, "We have not realized God.
How can we attain to peace?"

Thereupon the thought would flash in my mind:
"Why do they say so, am I then a superhuman being?
I never knew what worry was.
And the vision of God, it lies, as it were,
in the palm of my hand.
Whenever I like, I can have it."

Where will you find another like me?
See if you can find my peer.
Those who are given to contemplation on God
develop a subtle and pure mind.
Whatever object such a mind takes hold of,
it sticks to it tenaciously.
A flash of lightning is seen in a window pane,
but not in the wooden shutters.

Some having seen me involved in activities of the world,
have said that I am entangled in Maya.
But what to do, for I myself am Mahamaya.

People call me "Goddess" and I too am led to think so.
Or how could you explain all the strange things
that have happened in my life.
I should but think, "Let this happen" or "I shall eat this,"
and the Lord somehow fulfills these.

I am your Guru;
I know whether you are making progress or not.
How can you understand it, but you will achieve everything.

Most obstacles to worship are not external; they are internal.
They will gradually fall off one after another
by taking the Master's name and by meditation.

Do your duty and keep the mind on God.
Don't pay attention to whether the blemishes of the mind

are persisting or not, for we are behind you.
You all have come to me because you are all my own.
If one is the "very own" of another,
they remain inseparably connected in successive cycles of time.
I have indeed taken your responsibility.

Don't be afraid, have no fear — now you have been reborn.
I am assuming the fruits of all the deeds of your past lives.
Now you are pure, you are free of sin.

I have taken charge of everything, good and bad.
Can you understand everything I say?
If you could it would lighten my burden immensely.
I simply cannot put aside those whom I have accepted as my own.

I have done much more than necessary to make my life a model.
Ah, the ecstasy of those days!
On moonlit nights I would look at the moon
and pray with folded hands,
"May my heart be as pure as the rays of yonder moon!" or,
"Lord, there is a stain even in the moon,
but let there not be the least trace of stain in my mind."

I have been suffering from ailments for the last years.
I do not know for whose sins I have been suffering in this body.
Otherwise, how is it possible for me to get any disease?

But the body is one thing and the soul is another.
The soul pervades the whole body;

therefore I have been feeling this pain in my leg.
If I should withdraw my mind from the knee,
then I would not feel any pain there.

What shall I do, my dear?
My children come eagerly and take initiation.
But some do nothing regularly; some others do nothing at all.
I have taken up their burden, should I not look after them?

And so I do japa for them.
I pray to the Master on their behalf;
"Lord, arouse their spiritual consciousness and give them liberation.
The world is a well of sorrow and misery.
See to it that they do not have to come to it again."

The Master told me, "Whoever takes refuge in you,
I shall take him by the hand in the last moments
and lead him along the path."

In truth, I am your real Mother, not just the wife of your Guru,
nor an adopted mother or a stepmother either.
I am the Mother of all!
Whenever any disturbing thought comes to you, think of me.

I am the mother of the wicked, as I am the mother of the virtuous.
Never fear, and whenever you are in distress
just say to yourself, "I have a mother."

If you do not want to stay, then you can come with me.

When the time comes, all will have to go.
When the time comes, I will come and carry you along with me.

Make it a point always to remember whose child you are,
and who has granted refuge to you.
Whenever any evil thought haunts you, tell your mind:
"Being Her child, can I stoop so low as to indulge in such activity?"
You will find that you gain strength and peace of mind.

How can everyone recognize divinity, my dear?
There laid a diamond at a bathing place.
Taking it as an ordinary stone,
people rubbed the soles of their feet against it
after their bath to remove the dead skin.

One day a jeweler went there.
Seeing the stone, he immediately recognized
that it was a big precious diamond.
Taking it, he became rich and his problems were over.

The other incarnations survived their spiritual consorts.
Sri Ramakrishna left me behind this time
for demonstrating the ideal of Motherhood to the world.

Whenever I touch anything at home, I remember you.
I often think of those of you who are with me,
and for those who are far away, I say to the Master,
"O Lord, please look after them."
Let all be happy, and I shall suffer for them.

Mother on Sri Ramakrishna

"Sri Ramakrishna is everything —
both Guru and Ishtam."

Ganga, Gita, Gayatri, Bhagavata, Bhakta, Bhagavan,
Sri Ramakrishna, Sri Ramakrishna!

What shall I instruct you about?
The words of Sri Ramakrishna have been recorded in books.
If you can follow even one of His instructions
you will attain to everything in this life.
Always remember that the Master is the only protector.
If you forget this, you will have trouble.

The words of Sri Ramakrishna are true — every one of them.
You should know that people's consciousness
will not be awakened unless His words see the light of day.

Lay the burden of your mind before Sri Ramakrishna.
Tell Him your sorrows with your tears.
Pray to Sri Ramakrishna,
"Oh Lord, please forgive me of all sins
committed in this life and in previous lives."

Sri Ramakrishna was a perfect soul.
Certainly one can be free of transgressions
by confessing them to one like Him.
By remembering Sri Ramakrishna one gets rid of all sufferings.
By meditating on Him one gets all the spiritual moods.

Don't you see that all His devotees are happy?
Elsewhere you will not find devotees like those of the Master.
Here in Benares, I see so many holy men;
but can you point out one who is like His devotees?

Satya Yuga has begun since the birth of the Master.
Many luminaries have accompanied Him.
Naren was the chief among the seven sages.
Arjuna came as Yogen.

How many great souls can there be?
Sour mangoes can be had without number
but the good variety are rare.

Countless ordinary people take birth and die.
But only these jewels among men
come along with the Incarnation
for the sake of His mission.

This time the Master has come to save all —
the rich and the poor, the wise and the foolish.
Now there is a special Malaya breeze.
Just set your sail a little, take refuge in Him
and you will be blessed.

Why should you be fearful and helpless?
Does not the Master guide you through good and bad?
Why should you be so worried?
I have deposited you at His holy feet.
You will have to move about in that circle; you can't go beyond it.
He is always protecting you.

The Master used to say that His devotees are parts of Him —
his arms, legs, hair and other portions.
Those who are His, are His companions age after age.

My child, He alone is father and mother.
He alone has become our father and mother.
What will we gain by supernatural visions.
For us the Master exists — and He is everything.
Anyone who has once called upon the Master
with sincere faith and devotion, has nothing more to fear.

One who calls upon Him, by His grace gets Prema-bhakti.
This love is to be cherished in utmost privacy.

Ah, my dear, can one experience such delight everyday?
Everything is real, nothing is untrue.
The Master is all — He is Prakriti, He is Purusha.
Through Him you will achieve everything.

The Master told me that He would live three hundred years
in the subtle body, in the hearts of the devotees.
He further said that He would have many devotees
among white people.

Sri Ramakrishna said that He would reveal Himself
to all who took shelter under Him —
reveal Himself at least on their last day.
He will draw all to Him.

Why, my dear children,
did Sri Ramakrishna come only to eat rasagollas?
Come, child, come inside.
You have understood what sin is
and you are repentant of your deeds.
Come, I shall initiate you.
Surrender everything at the feet of Sri Ramakrishna.
Why should you fear?

How fine His teachings are!
What a great soul was born!
How many people are being illumined by His words!
He was the embodiment of bliss itself.

If you pray to the Master before His picture
then He Himself manifests through that picture.
The place where His picture is kept becomes a shrine.
The Master Himself will pay special attention to such a place.

The Master partakes of the food which is offered to Him.
A light comes out of His eyes and licks all the articles of food.
His ambrosial touch replenishes them again
so there is no decrease.

The Master does not require any food.
He eats the offering only for the gratification of the devotees.
The sacred prasada purifies the heart.
The mind becomes impure by eating food
without first offering it to God.

Look here, I never felt that the Master practiced all the religions
with the express intention of teaching the harmony of all religions.
He was always immersed in God-consciousness.
Renunciation was His crown.

He followed all the disciplines —
those of Christians, Muslims, Vaishnavas, etc. —
for the sake of God-realization,
and He enjoyed the lila in different ways,
entirely unconscious of how time passed.

But still, do you know, my dear, in this age,
renunciation has been His specialty.
Has anyone ever seen at any time
that kind of spontaneous renunciation?

Do not make any distinction between Sri Ramakrishna and me.
Pray to the particular aspect of divinity revealed to you.
Worship ends with absorption in meditation.
Start here in the heart and end here in the head.

Neither mantra or scripture is of any avail.
Bhakti, devotion, accomplishes everything.

Sri Ramakrishna is everything — both Guru and Ishtam.
He is all in all.

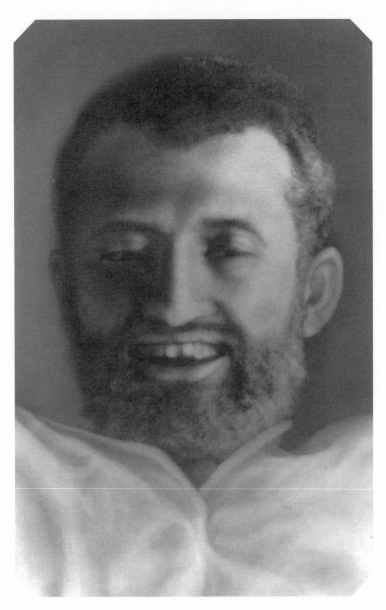

Devotees and Luminaries

"The inner soul feels for a sincere devotee."

My precious spiritual children, may you attain devotion to God.
Even the impossible becomes possible through devotion.
The inner soul feels for a sincere devotee.

Many may take the name of God after becoming hardened
by the contaminating influence of the world,
but that one alone is blessed who is devoted to God
from very childhood.

There are two classes of devotees.
One class devotes itself to the service of God,
like here on earth.
The other remains immersed in meditation for ages.

The Ishvarakoti can gather back the mind from formless meditation
and direct it to the relative plane of consciousness.
Not all can do this.
Only the Paramahamsa can.
A hamsa can separate milk from a mixture of milk and water
and drink only the milk.

Immersed in meditation, the enlightened ones remain as they are,
like wooden statues, for ages.
When God needs them, He brings them down
from their respective places.

The Master said that He brought Naren down
from the plane of the Seven Sages.

His words are verily the words of the Vedas.
They can never be untrue.

There are different types of perfect souls:
perfect from birth, perfect through spiritual disciplines,
perfect through the grace of the teacher
and made perfect all of a sudden.

One could be born with a pure mind
if one had performed austerities
and spiritual practices in a previous birth.
He who has a pure mind sees everything pure.

Some of the Ishvarakotis are immersed in the world
with families and children.
They are rotting there, perhaps they have some desires.

But let me tell you one thing,
there is a great complexity in this creation.
The Master does one thing through one person
and another thing through another man.

Oh, it is so inscrutable!
But even a householder can be an Ishvarakoti.
What is the harm?

Why can't one lead a good life if one is married?
The mind alone is everything.
Did not the Master marry me?

What else can you do
if you do not believe in the words of high-souled beings?
Is there any other way
than the one trodden by sages and seers
and other holy personages?

Can everybody recognize an incarnation?
One or two persons only can recognize Him.
How much suffering do they undergo
for the liberation of human beings.

Even when the Master used to vomit blood,
in His final illness,
He never stopped speaking.
He was all the while worried
about the well-being of the people.

Japa And Meditation

"Don't just seek God, see God."

It is evening.
Come, my children.

Instead of meditating you are gossiping!
Can anything worthwhile ever be attained by sitting idle?

There should be a regular time for practice of japa and meditation,
for no one knows when the auspicious moment will come.
It comes suddenly — one has no hint of it beforehand.
Therefore, regularity in spiritual practice should be observed,
no matter how busy one may be with worldly duties.

Practice meditation regularly, for your mind is still unripe.
After prolonged practice of meditation
your mind will become steady.

It is harmful if the mind is drawn to worldly objects
like money and members of one's family.
Nonetheless, the mind naturally dwells on one's daily activities.

So you should constantly discriminate
between the real and the unreal.
Know the worldly objects to which the mind is drawn to be unreal
and surrender your mind to God.

The practice of meditation
will lead your mind to such one-pointedness
that you won't like to give up meditation.
But when you do not achieve such concentration of mind,
don't force yourself to meditation.

On such occasions finish your spiritual practice
by simply saluting the Lord.
That day on which you have the right mood,
you will have meditation spontaneously.

Whether you jump in the water or are pushed in from behind,
your cloth will get soaked nevertheless.
Devotion will come if you make the mind one-pointed.

So, every morning and evening

perform japa and meditation with a cool brain.
It is not an easy task.
Compared to meditation, it is easier to till a plot of land.

The mind will be steadied if one repeats the name of God
fifteen to twenty-thousand times a day.
I myself have experienced it.
Let them practice it first: if they fail, let them complain.

One should practice japa with some devotion,
but this is not done.
They will not do anything, but only complain, saying,
"Why do I not succeed?"

Can one have the vision of God everyday?
Does an angler catch a big carp everyday,
the moment he sits with his rod?
Arranging everything about him, he sits and concentrates.

Once in a while a big carp swallows the hook.
Many a time he is disappointed.
Don't relax the practices for that reason.
Do more japa and meditate.

Why can't one meditate if one has a pure mind?
Don't just seek God, see God!
Why should one not be able to see God?
One should practice japa and meditation at regular times,
giving up idleness.

When a pure soul performs japa,
the holy name bubbles up spontaneously from within.
There is no effort to repeat the name.

If you don't succeed in meditation,
practice japa, for japa leads to perfection.
If a meditative mood sets in, well and good.
If not, don't force your mind to meditate.

Japa leads to success, but one must practice.
Once I heard that an American cowboy
used to carry a calf in his arms everyday to a far off grazing field.
The calf gradually grew into an ox.

Still he could carry the ox
and used to surprise others by his great strength.
All this is the outcome of practice.

In the same way, man achieves the highest goal
through the practice of japa.
God has given us fingers
that they may be blessed by repeating His Name.
So be content in all circumstances and take His Name.

If you keep count while you do japa,
your mind will be drawn to the counting.
So do japa without counting.

As the timepiece on the wall goes on ticking

So too must you continue to repeat God's Name.
Thus you will attain everything.
Nothing else need be done.

I tell the beads for all those whose names I can recall.
And for those whom I cannot remember,
I pray to the Master saying,
"Thakur, I have so many children in various places.
I cannot remember the names of many of them.
You kindly look after them — kindly look after their well-being."

Remembrance of God's Name helps one this much —
instead of losing a leg
one may suffer merely from a thorn entering one's foot.
But remember, if the mantra is not pronounced correctly,
it takes more time to achieve any result.
For this and other matters, consult a Guru.

The Guru

"He who warns in time is a true friend."

It is easy to break.
How many can build?
How many can show others the right path?

Mankind is prone to weakness.
He who warns in time is a true friend.
What is the use in saying "Ah"
when the right time has passed.

It is no doubt that teaching is a noble profession,
but it is not meant for all.
Is it an easy thing to teach?

All teachers are one.
The same power of God works through them all.
But the giver of the mantra is the real Guru,
for by repetition of this mantra
one obtains dispassion and renunciation.

The word of the mantra is living.
Is it ever possible to give it back?
Can one, once having felt attraction to Guru,
get rid of him?

Some day in the future
they will come around
and fall at the feet of the Guru
whom they now abuse.

Power passes through the mantra —
the Guru's goes to the disciple
and the disciple's goes to the Guru.

That is why the Guru
at the time of initiation
takes on the sins of the disciple
and suffers from physical maladies.

It is extremely difficult to be a Guru.
If the disciple commits a sin,
the Guru has to suffer as well.
On the other hand,
the Guru is benefited if the disciple is good.

It is not wise that a Guru and his disciple live together,
for then a disciple observes the life and activities of his Guru
and very often takes his Guru to be a mere human being.
This causes harm to the disciple.

One must have reverence for one's Guru.
You should not doubt the words of your own teacher.
One's chance for salvation lies in reverence for him.

It would be good if the disciple could live
in a place close to the guru's residence
and spend some time daily in visiting his guru,
enjoying his company and receiving his instructions.

Once a disciple uttering "Jai Guru" with great faith,
crossed a river by walking on water.
Observing this, the guru mused,
"My name has so much power!"
Then uttering "I, I," the guru went into the water —
and was drowned.

What do you need an Incarnation for?
One's own guru is far superior to even an incarnation of God.
Try to understand this and keep steady.

Karma

"Everyone reaps the effects of their own actions."

Human being —
today it is, tomorrow it is not.
No one will accompany a person after death.
Only actions — good and bad — follow, even after death.

Karma alone is responsible for our misery and happiness.
The result of karma is inevitable,
but by repeating the name of God you can lessen its intensity.

If you were destined to have a wound as wide as a ploughshare,
you will get a pinprick at least.
Karma's effect can be counteracted greatly by japa and austerities.

One cannot blame God for all the sins committed.
It is true that He has become all living beings,
but everyone reaps the effects of their actions.
No doubt the sun is one, but its shining varies
according to the place and objects it illumines.

Many a time a man takes birth and dies, again and again,
in a certain family due to his karma.
But no one will suffer for all time.
Every action brings its own result,
and one gets one's opportunities accordingly.

That you have been born in this age is a great blessing.
This is the time when you can see His divine sport.
One can easily see this divine play
if one looks upon it with faith and devotion.

Realization and Liberation

"Those who have come here,
those who are my children,
have already achieved liberation."

I bless you on this holy day
that you may attain liberation in this life.
Birth and death are extremely painful.
May you not suffer from them anymore.

The aim of life is to realize God
and remain immersed in the contemplation of His holy feet always.
He is watching over your earthly life as well as your life to come.

Can anyone think of God all the time?
Spend some time relaxing
and some time absorbed in thoughts of Him.

What all seek when they come to me —
is it any greens or fish
that you could buy it by paying so much price?

But you, being my child, can you ever be doomed?
Those who have come here, those who are my children,
have already achieved liberation.
Even God can do no harm to my children!

Only those who belong to a high spiritual category
can become monks and gain liberation from all kinds of fetters.
Some, again, are born just to enjoy the world.
I say that it is good to finish in entirety enjoyments and sufferings.
But it was different in the case of the companions of the Master.

My child, have no fear.
Suppose you are asleep on a cot
and somebody removes you along with the cot to another place.
Will you realize where you are immediately upon awaking?
Not at all.
Only when the drowsiness clears away completely
will you realize that you have come to a new place.

For how many cycles did the munis and the rishis of old
practice austerities in order to realize God,

and you believe you will attain to Him in a flash?
If not in this life you will attain Him in the next.
Is it so easy to realize God?
But this time the Master has shown an easy path;
therefore it will be possible for all to realize God.

God and His Grace

"Everything depends upon the grace of God."

For realization, the grace of God is needed.
One should then make oneself fit for the grace of God.
Everything depends upon the grace of God.
He bestows His grace upon anyone He likes.
Grace is the important thing.

Nothing can happen without the will of God.
Not even a blade of grass can move.
When a man passes into a favorable time,
he gets the desire to contemplate God.

But when the time is unfavorable,
he gets all the facilities for doing evil actions.
Everything happens in time according to the will of God.

In the fullness of spiritual realization,
one will find that He who resides in one's heart,
resides in the hearts of others as well —
the oppressed, the persecuted, the untouchable and the outcast.
This realization makes one truly humble.

Please do not worry so much, my child.
Let the will of God be done.
You have been following the right path.
The Lord will never put you to any great difficulty.
One may get grace instantaneously
through the grace of a great soul.

My children, please do not weep.
You are living gods and goddesses.
Who is able to renounce all for His sake?

Even the injunctions of destiny are canceled
if one takes refuge in God.
Destiny strikes off with her own hand
what she has written about such a person.

What does a man become by realizing God?
Does he get two horns?
No.
What happens is, he develops discrimination
between the real and the unreal,
gets illumination and goes beyond life and death.

God is realized in Spirit.
How else can one see God?
Has God talked to anybody devoid of ecstatic fervor?
One sees God in spiritual vision, talks to Him,
and establishes a relationship with Him in Spirit.

Can you tell me who has seen God?
One may get a vision in a dream,
but to see God in physical form is a matter of rare good fortune.

It is God alone who has become father and mother.
God alone looks after us.
Otherwise, where were you and where are you now?

Your parents brought you up,
but at last you realized that you do not belong to them.

Who but God can say what is going on
in the remote planes of existence?
It is only God that can be omniscient in this realm of Maya.
Perhaps there are no other beings
on those distant planets and stars.

God cannot be realized through japa, worship or meditation.
God is only realized through His grace.
Nonetheless, one must perform japa and meditation,
for they remove the impurities of one's mind.
God's grace then becomes revealed.

As one gets the fragrance of a flower by handling it
or the scent of sandalwood by rubbing it against a stone,
one becomes spiritually awakened
by continuously contemplating God.
But you can become illumined right now if you become desireless.

DESIRES

*"Desire is at the root of all sorrows,
the cause of repeated births and deaths,
and the main obstacle on the path of liberation."*

Can you tell me what object is to be prayed for from God?
Is it wisdom, devotion, objects that make you happy in life?
To say in one word, we must pray for *nirvasana,*
freedom from desire.

Desire is at the root of all sorrows,
the cause of repeated births and deaths,
and the main obstacle on the path of liberation.

Desire may be compared to a tiny seed.
It is like a big banyan tree
growing out of a seed that is no bigger than a dot.
As long as human beings have desires,
there is no end to transmigration.
It is desire alone that takes them from one body to another.

Once I visited the image of Jagannath
at the time of the car festival.
I wept in joy to see so many having the vision of the deity
and thought to myself,
"It is good — they will all be saved."

But later on I realized it was not so.
Only one or two who were absolutely free of desires
could attain liberation.

The Ishvarakotis are *purna kama* —
they have all their desires fulfilled in God.
Therefore they have no worldly desires.

Love for the sake of divine Love is not possible
so long as a man has any desire.

Not all can free themselves from desires.
The creation is going on because all cannot be free of desires.
People with desires take their births again and again.

Though one gets a new body on account of desires,
yet one does not completely lose spiritual consciousness
if one has one's credit merits from previous births.

All people, excepting highly advanced souls,
live in a spirit body for a year after death.
The spirit body is like a body made of air.

Afterwards they go to other planes
and experience pleasure and pain
and in course of time are born again
in human forms according to their desires.

Others attain salvation from those planes.
After a birth in a human body, some attain salvation in this life,
whereas others take inferior births
to reap the results of their karma.

That is indeed the last birth
in which one gets rid of all desires completely.
The last birth means that one will not have to come again.
This life marks the end of all that.

Whether or not the person has desires in his present state,
the Master has foreseen that in the end,
all the desires will leave such a person.
In some cases, it is possible that the mind
will become absolutely bereft of all desires just before death.

My children who still have desires, why do you worry so much?
The desires of your mind — you must first fulfill them.
Later on you will attain the eternal peace of Ramakrishna Loka.
The Master has created a new kingdom for all of you.

There are two kinds of desires:
one that stimulates enjoyment
and the other that quickens dispassion.

In the case of the devotees, there are no real desires.
They are nothings.
They are mere fancies that appear and disappear in your mind.
The more they come and go the better for you.

About desires in the mind,
the Master will grant only those which you really need
and which will bring you good.
Continue to practice as you are doing now.
Why fear? We are with you.

So many children come or write to me,
but I notice that they have so many desires.
Some say, "I pray so much, meditate,
and tell so many beads and yet nothing happens."

Others complain about the anxieties,
fears, wants, diseases and sorrows of this world.
I cannot hear any more of this — where is their yearning?

They speak so much of their devotion
and earnestness on the one hand,
and on the other they are so pleased
with any little enjoyment they may come to have and say,
"Ah, how merciful is He!"
That is the measure of their devotional hankering.

Will they abstain from desire because of my prohibition
if their desires are strong?
And to those who have understood by virtue of great merit
that all this is Maya's play,
and believe that God alone is Reality,
should I not offer a little help and encouragement?
Is there any end to the miseries of the world?

The World and Worldliness

"The less you become attached to the world,
the more you enjoy peace of mind."

My children, the world is a great mire.
If one gets into it, he finds it difficult to get free.
Even Brahma and Vishnu gasp in it,
what to speak of mankind.

There is no happiness whatsoever in human birth.
The world is verily filled with misery.
Happiness here is only a name.

Those on whom the grace of the Master has fallen,
alone know Him to be God Himself.
And remember, that is the only happiness.

The happiness of the world is transitory.
The less you become attached to the world,
the more you enjoy peace of mind.

At the time of creation,
people were born with the quality of sattva, light.
They had wisdom from their very birth.

Consequently, they at once realized
the unreal nature of the world.
They renounced it and practiced austerity.
They were liberated in no time.

The Creator found that the purpose of His creation
was going to be frustrated.
These wise ones who were thus liberated,

were unfit for the continuance of the play of the world.
Then He again started the work of creation
and mixed the qualities of rajas and tamas with the sattva.
Thus His purpose was fulfilled.

How many kinds of people there are — who can say?
For those who live in society,
there is no end to fear.

You see, my children,
the worldly-minded belong to a different class.
They will again and again come to this world
and go rotting in their worldly life.
If at any time they are blessed by God,
only then can they be liberated.

The worldly-minded crave for money and money only.
Never have they prayed for knowledge or devotion,
even mistakenly.
Well, let them have what they seek.

What is there in money, my dear?
The Master could not even touch money.
His hand used to curl back when any metal contacted him.

He used to say,
"The world is an illusion.
Ah, Ramlal, if I felt that the world was real,
I would have covered your Kamarpukur in gold.

But I knew it was an illusion.
God alone is real."

Everything, husband, wife,
even the body, is only illusory.
These are all shackles of illusion.
Unless you can free yourself from these bondages,
you will never be able to go
to the other shore of the world.

Even this body,
the identification of the self with the body, must go.
What is this body, my darling?
It is nothing but three pounds of ash when it is cremated.
Why so much vanity about it?

Do you think that you can get rid of lust altogether?
It will be there in some form or other
as long as the body lasts.
But then, I tell you, after taking refuge in God
it will be reduced to a state comparable
to a charmed snake.

There are many who are miserable
in spite of their wealth.
The rich should serve God and His devotees with money,
and the poor worship God by repeating His name.

My relatives have enjoyed my company so much
and still they do not show the least glimmer of wisdom.

They are like bamboo or silk-cotton trees.
Even if they grow close to a sandalwood tree,
what will it profit them?
The trees must have some essence.

You see, the devotion of worldly people
is like a drop of water on a red hot frying pan;
It evaporates in no time at all.

But my child, what is worldly life to you?
For you, worldly life is as good as living under a tree.
Besides, is this life separate from God?

He is everywhere.
Be content with whatever
and in whatever situation He places you.
The goal is to call upon Him and attain to Him.

In the old days, many great disciples used to come.
Those who come nowadays simply keep on saying,
"Give us a vision of the Master."
They do no spiritual practice, no japa, no meditation.
God knows how many wicked things
they have done in their past.

Only after terrible sufferings does a being resort finally to God.
Selfishness, well, that persists
as long as a person is self-assertive,
and disappears when that is overcome.
But why fear?

All conditions can turn favorable by the will of the Master.
He used to say that avidya maya is more powerful than vidya.
That is why avidya maya has kept the world enchanted.

Misery and Suffering

"My children,
work to remove the sufferings of the world."

The sufferings of people bound in the world
pain me very much.
But what can I do, my child?
They will not seek liberation.

Have you seen the mother crab?
It peeps out of its hole again and again,
but then goes down again.
It struggles hard repeatedly to free itself, but fails.

Why is that?
Because of her numerous progeny living in the hole.
Attraction drags her down in spite of all her efforts.
Such is the case of worldly people as well.

A man in the street whose consciousness is not awakened
is quite happy.
But those whose consciousness is partially awakened
and who want to realize God,
suffer a great deal if they do not see Him.

The ordinary people are quite happy.
They eat, drink and make merry.
Will they ever be satiated?
Only the devotees know no end of suffering.

Are the worldly people ever satiated with enjoyments?
Nothing can satisfy them;
no, not even if they have plenty.

And yet they always spin out the tale of their woes.
But joy and sorrow, where will they go?
They are our companions.

Everybody says regretfully,
"There is so much misery in the world.
We have prayed so much to God,
but still there is no end of misery."
But misery is only the gift of God.
It is the symbol of His compassion.

My children, work to remove the sufferings of the world.
The purpose of one's life is fulfilled
only when one is able to bring joy to another.

The Master and I have suffered on account of coming to earth.
Those who came to us expecting worldly gain
have disappeared saying,
"Ah, He is an incarnation of God!
How can He be ill?
This is all Maya."
But those who are our own
have been suffering a great deal in seeing our misery.

So long as the ego exists,
desires will undoubtedly remain.
But those desires will not hurt you
if you let the Master be your protector.
You must live in a spirit of service and self-surrender to Him.

Service and Compassion

"To serve is the highest religion"

Most holy beings have an aura of grandeur around them.
Attracted by that, many come to serve them
and remain intoxicated by that grandeur.
This will cause their downfall.
How many can serve holy beings
with the proper attitude?

Everyone should serve their parents,
particularly those of you
who have come here together to serve all people.
Forbearance is a great virtue.
No other quality is greater than this.

You will play a true role of a son
only if you can help your mother acquire the means
for her higher evolution in the hereafter.
Never forget that you have grown up
sucking the milk of her breasts.

Remember with what difficulty she tended you.
To serve her is the highest religion.
It would be different, of course,
if she stands in the way of your progress towards God.

Can you call him a man who is devoid of compassion?
He is a veritable beast.
Sometimes I forget myself in compassion.
Then I do not remember who I am.

Those indeed are unfortunate
who do not gain my compassion.
I do not know anyone, not even an insect,
for whom I do not feel compassion.

Today a beggar came to the ashram
The monks would not stir themselves and became irritated
Did you notice their insensitivity and hear their remarks?
They have driven the poor man away.
They could not shake off their idleness and give him something.

He only wanted a handful of rice.
And they could not take the trouble to do this bit of work.
Whenever you have some money in hand or can help,
feed the poor, some holy persons or give to a spiritual cause.

Is it proper to deprive a man of what is his due?
Even to the cow we owe these peelings of the vegetables.
We should hold these near her mouth.

Food

"First, offer to God whatever you eat."

I eat through the mouths of all of you, my dears.
Your eating is as good as my taking food.
How much I have eaten since coming to the circle of the Master.

My dears, there are certain dangers involved
in eating together with others from the same plate,
in lying on the same bed with another,
and in using somebody else's cloth or bath-towel.

Also, a person's good or bad physical condition
may be transferred to the body of another.
Therefore be careful.

My child, your body is also my body.
I suffer if you do not keep good health.

Eating food that has not been offered
is equivalent to eating sin.
The place and manner in which it is prepared
is also important.

So, first, offer to God whatever you eat.
One must not eat unoffered food.
As your food is, so will be your blood.

From pure food you will get pure blood,
pure mind and strength.
Pure mind begets prema, ecstatic love.

The Mind

"It is pure mind that shows man the path"

My child, the mind is like a wild elephant.
It races with the wind.
Therefore one should discriminate all of the time.
One should work hard for the realization of God.

The wind alone makes the candle flame flicker.
In similar fashion,
fancies and desires make the mind restless.
Repeat the holy Name and the mind will become steady.

The mind is by nature restless.
Therefore, at the outset, to make the mind steady,
one may practice meditation by regulating the breath a little.
That helps steady the mind.

But one must not overdo it for that heats the brain.
You may talk of the vision of God or of meditation,
but remember, the mind is everything.
One gets everything when the mind becomes steady.

You should certainly repeat the mantra.
However, calling on God with one's mind steadfast
is equivalent to a million repetitions of the mantra.

What is the good of doing japa all day
if there is no concentration of the mind.
Collectedness of mind is essential,
then only His grace descends.

You see, it is the nature of water to flow downward,
but the sun's rays lift it up towards the sky;
likewise it is the very nature of the mind to go to lower things,
to objects of enjoyment,
but the grace of God can make the mind
go towards higher things.

As you turn the direction of the wicked mind,
that mind itself will be able to grasp the chosen deity.
When worldly thoughts crop up in your mind and possess it,
then you should go away from the company of others
and pray to Him with tears in your eyes.
He will remove all the dross from the mind,
and will also give you understanding.

About the weaknesses of the mind, it is nature's law, my child.
Just as you find the full moon and the new moon,
the mind is possessed of noble thoughts at times
and haunted by evil thoughts at other moments.

An impure mind does not easily become pure.
The more you emphasize your obsession,
the more obsessed you become.
It is true of all things.

Unless Mahamaya opens the way,
nothing will happen by any means.
How many can do japa and meditation all the time?

Did you notice the other day how one man
forcibly did more japa than he could stand
and got his mind deranged?

If the mind is gone, what remains?
It is like the thread of a screw.
If one thread is loose the fellow becomes mad
or falls into the trap of Mahamaya and thinks himself very clever.
On the other hand, if it is tightened the right way,
one goes along the correct path and obtains peace and bliss.

Is the mind the cause of troubles only?
Even when you try to attain to Brahman,
you shall have to carry with you the mind too.
At the present stage the assistance of the mind is very necessary.
It is the pure mind that shows man the path.

Spiritual Practice
and Austerities

*"All practice this and that discipline
because they think that it is their duty to do so.
But how many seek God?"*

Where is that competent student
who can understand spiritual instruction?
First of all, one should be fit;
otherwise, the instructions prove futile.

At least once at dawn and once at dusk
one must sit down for spiritual practices.
It is like the rudder of a ship.

When you sit at dusk,
then you get to think of all that you have done
and not done during the day.

Then you have to compare the states of your mind
yesterday and today.
Then, doing japa,
one has to meditate on the form of one's Ishta.

Let those who complain of mental worry do what I did.
Let them get up at three o'clock in the morning
and sit for meditation.
Let me see whether they can still have any worry of mind.

They will not, however, do that,
but can only talk about their troubles.
Just look at all these girls.
They never listen to me.
Such disobedience.

Austerities, pilgrimage, worship, the earning of money —
one should do all these things in the days of youth.
In old age the body deteriorates.
It does not possess any strength.
The mind loses its vigor.
Is it possible to do anything at that time?

It is quite right that the young sannyasins of our Math
have been directing their minds to God from an early age.
This is the right time for them to do so.

My child, austerities and worship,
practice all these things right now.
Will these things be possible later on?
Whatever you want to achieve, achieve now;
this is the right time.

Can the mango which ripens out of season
be as sweet as the one which ripens in the proper season?
Men are trying to get fruit out of season.
This is true of spiritual life as well.

Perhaps one practices japa and austerity in this life.
In the next life one intensifies the spiritual mood
and in the following advances it further,
and thus spiritual evolution goes on.

The moment that one's karma comes to an end one realizes God.
That is one's last birth.
This plus the practice of spiritual discipline and time
are the factors in the attainment of spiritual knowledge.

Yet, since God is our own,
He can reveal Himself to His devotees by His mere will.
But who has this faith that He is one's own?
All practice this and that discipline
because they think it is their duty to do so.
But how many seek God?

What good are asanas and breathing exercises
if the mind becomes concentrated on its own?
Asanas and pranayama endow one with occult powers
and these lead a man astray.

If you practice asana too much
then the mind becomes attached to the body.

Yet, a man's body becomes unwell
if physical exercise is given up.
Therefore take exercise.
May you be illumined!

As to those who surrender themselves to God
but practice no spiritual disciplines,
that they surrender themselves to God,
placing implicit trust in Him, that is their spiritual discipline.

All that you have to do is to pay obeisance to God
at the end of the day.
If one firmly takes ahold of an idea,
one doesn't have to perform any other discipline.

Spiritual progress becomes easier
if husband and wife agree in their views
regarding spiritual practices.
Otherwise there will be discord in the household.

For the sake of God-realization,
a married person may live a life of self-control.
It is certainly no sin
One must control the senses.

One may also practice self-control
after the birth of one or two children.
And such a one may also give up the world
after making provision for one's dependents.

So perform japa with love, sincerity and self-surrender.
Then meditate on the Lord.
Remember how helpless you are in this world
and slowly begin sadhana as directed by your Guru.

Some believe that having faith in the Guru is enough,
and that is true.
But the point is this:
the house may have all kinds of food-stuff for cooking,
but one must cook them and take the meal.
He who cooks earlier gets his meal earlier too.

Some eat in the morning, some in the evening,
and there are yet others who starve
because they are lazy and reluctant to cook.
The more arduously one practices spiritual disciplines,
the more quickly one will attain God.

Through spiritual practices, the ties of past karma are cut asunder.
But the realization of God cannot be achieved
without ecstatic love for Him.
Do you know the significance of japa and other spiritual practices?
By these, the dominance of the sense organs is subdued.

The men and women who have come to the Master and I
have not assembled for fun.
Every one of them is doing spiritual disciplines.
They know that they are extremely fortunate
in getting this human birth.

Have intense devotion to God.
One must work hard.
How can one achieve anything without effort?
One must devote some time for prayer
even in the midst of household duties.

Work

"People renounce the world to repeat God's name but get entangled in the world nevertheless."

Always be engaged in some work or other.
It will be conducive to the health of both the body and the mind.
One must do some work.

Through work alone can one remove the bondage of work,
not by avoiding work.
Total detachment comes later on.
One should not be without work even for a moment.

If the mind is kept engaged in some kind of work,
it doesn't engage in silly thoughts.
But if you sit idle,
the mind is likely to indulge in various kinds of thoughts.

A man eager to keep away from acidic foods
builds a home under a tamarind tree, as the proverb goes.
People renounce the world to repeat God's name
but get entangled in activities nevertheless.

About your spiritual duties, people no doubt say
that pilgrimages during inauspicious times are prohibited.
One can postpone a holy duty out of considerations of time.
But look,
death takes no notice of time.
Since death has no fixed hours,
one should perform holy duties as soon as an opportunity arises.

Some complain that work at the ashram or monastery
keeps one too busy to find time

for regularly performing japa and meditation.
But whose work are you doing?
It is His work only.

Do I always remember my divine nature?
Is it possible always?
If it were so, can all this work go on?
Yet amidst all this work, whenever the desire arises,
inspiration comes in a flash upon a little thought
and the whole of the play of Mahamaya comes to be understood.

All action belongs to Her, so work should be done carefully.
The sweeping is finished and you throw the broom away?
Everything should be given its due respect.
A broom, though unclean itself, still cleans dirty places.

My dear, take notice of your surroundings when you move about
and you should also keep yourself informed
of everything that happens at the place where you live.
But do not gossip about it.

Faultfinding

*"You might have done good to a man a thousand times,
and harmed him only once;
he will turn away from you for that one offense."*

The mind is everything.
It is in the mind alone that one feels pure and impure.
A man, first of all, must make his own mind guilty
and then alone he can see another man's guilt.

Does anything ever happen to another
if you enumerate his faults?
It only injures you.
This has been my attitude since childhood.
Hence I cannot see anyone's faults.

If a man does a trifle for me,
I try to remember him even for that.
To see the faults of others!
One should never do it.
I never do so.
Forgiveness is Tapasya.

Man is bound to make mistakes.
One should not notice them.
If one does not follow this rule, it harms oneself alone.
By constantly observing the faults of others,
in the end one will become a mere fault-finder.

So I tell you this: If you want peace of mind
do not find fault with others.
Rather, see your own faults.
Learn to make the whole world your own.
No one is a stranger.
Indeed, the entire world is your very own.

In earlier days I also had an eye for people's faults.
Thereafter I wept before the Master, praying,
"O Master, I do not want to see anyone's faults,"
and thereby got rid of the habit.

You might have done good to a man a thousand times
and harmed him only once;
he will turn away from you for that one offense.
One should in fact note the merits.

Don't let your mind become disturbed over trifles.
It will make you forget the Lord.
Whatever people may say, remember the Master
and do what you consider to be correct.

Should one speak such words as would hurt another?
Even if it is truth,
it should not be told in an unpleasant manner.
Finally, you will end up with that kind of nature.
If one's sensitivity is lost,
then nothing will control one's speech.

Look, there is certainly what is called *Sevaparabdha* —
fault in serving.
That means, as one serves,
gradually one becomes more proud and egoistic,
and then one wants to make a puppet out of one's master.

Whether the master stands, eats or sits,
he must do so at the bidding of the attendant.
The attitude of true service entirely disappears from them.

The Master used to say,
"Look on people as mere worms."
By this He did not mean all kinds of people.
He was referring only to fault-finders
and people of mean tendencies,
not to those who worship the Lord.

Worship and Prayer

"Always remember that you have a Mother."

From time immemorial,
innumerable people have worshipped images
and thereby attained spiritual knowledge.
Do you want to deny this fact?
Sri Ramakrishna never cherished
any such parochial or one-sided view.

Brahman exists everywhere.
The prophets and incarnations are born
to show the way to benighted humanity.
They give different instructions suited to different temperaments.
There are many ways to realize the Truth.

One day, while living at Dakshineswar,
I made a big garland of seven strands
with some jasmine and rangam.
I soaked the garland in water in a stone bowl
and quickly the buds turned into full blossoms.

I sent the garland to the Kali temple
to adorn the image of the Divine Mother.
Sri Ramakrishna came to the temple.
He at once fell into an ecstatic mood to see the beauty of Kali
so much enhanced by the flowers.

Flowers are best used in the service of the Lord.
Otherwise it is better that they fade away on the trees.
I feel very bad when I see foppish gentlemen
make a bouquet of flowers
or sometimes casually put a flower to their nose and admire:
"Ah! What a fine scent!"
Oh dear, perhaps the very next moment they throw it on the floor
or trample it with booted feet.

The wicked do not feel the divine presence in the image.
The deity disappears, as it were, before them.
He can do what He likes by His mere will.
This also is a sport of God.

A worldly woman has come into the shrine.
Her husband is ill.
She has come here to pray for his recovery.

Instead of being prayerful and penitent,
she has covered herself with perfumes.
Does this become one who comes to a shrine?
Ah! Such is the nature of your modern people.

He who will pray to God eagerly will see Him.
To call upon Him at the conjunction of day and night
is most auspicious.

Night disappears and day arrives,
or day disappears and night arrives —
this is the conjunction of day and night.
The mind remains pure at these times.
How much intelligence does a man possess?
While praying, he is likely to ask for something
other than what he really needs.

It is wise to take refuge in God.
He will give whatever is necessary.
However, one should pray for devotion and desirelessness.
Such a prayer does no harm.

New devotees should be given the privilege
of service in the shrine room.
Their new zeal makes them serve the Lord carefully.
The others are tired of service.

Service, in the real sense of the word, is not a joke.
One should be extremely careful about making His service flawless.
But the truth is that God knows our foolishness and forgives us.
One must work in the shrine room with great attention.

Offerings, pranams and the rest
should be made at the proper time.

114

The scriptures prohibit making pranam
to a person who is ill or lying down.
Pranam in such a circumstance fixes the disease in the person.
Nobody should be saluted in their illness.

Look at these flowers with a blue color.
How can one decorate God without such fine flowers?
Bring more flowers!
Rakhal, Tarak, Sarat, Khoka, Yogen, Golap —
offer flowers in the names of each of them.

Offer flowers for the sake of all my known and unknown children.
May all be blessed in this world and the next.
And always remember that you have a Mother
Now come, my dear, and I will give you initiation.

Initiation and Mantra

"The true purpose of initiation is to try and realize God through sincere spiritual effort."

The true purpose of initiation is to try and realize God
through sincere spiritual self-effort.

The mantra also purifies the body.
Man becomes pure by repeating the mantra of God.
The body cannot be pure without initiation.

Whatever I have to give, I have given at the time of initiation.
If you want peace immediately, practice the prescribed disciplines.
Otherwise, you will get it only after the fall of the body.

And mark you, I have not given you the mantra.
It is the Master who has done so.
And He who is the Master, am I.

The human teacher utters the mantra into the ear,
but God breathes the Spirit into the soul.
Everything then depends upon one's mind.
Nothing can be achieved without the purity of mind.

A Guru may turn away a person
seeking to be a disciple time after time.
That one who is really eager for the blessing of the guru,
however, will come to him even by begging.

The truth is this:
He who is really anxious to cross the ocean of this world,
will somehow break his bonds.
No one can entangle him.

Financial difficulties, awaiting a reply, fear of going back unfulfilled,
these are mere excuses.

I give you initiation only because you are a noble soul.
See that you do not betray me.

You are perfectly satisfied if you get the sacred mantra
but you never think of the consequence.

A spiritual teacher has to suffer for the sins of his devotees.
Someone told me that I should not initiate so many beings,
but only those I could remember and keep in touch with.
But the Master never forbade me to do so.
I entrust the Master with their responsibility.

I pray to Him every day to look after them.
Besides, do you know that the Master Himself
taught me these mantras?
He gave me mantras possessing great power.
They are imbued with the power of renunciation.

Renunciation

"Forgetting your personality,
try to realize your identity with God."

About renunciation,
you will acquire it slowly.
You will make some progress in this life and more in the next.

It is the body alone that changes, the Atman remains the same.
So wherever you live, you must feel quite at home.
And please practice renunciation a little.

Worldly people cannot even give up
their attachment to a brass pot;
how could they then think of renouncing the world?

Householders need not have external renunciation.
Internal renunciation will come to them of itself.
But some people need external renunciation as well.

An unmarried person who leads a pure life
will advance towards God with rapid strides.
Others, tied hand and foot,
find it impossible to extricate themselves from the world.

Yet, some monks may become very vain.
They may think, "See, he does not respect me.
He does not bow down before me" and so on.
Thus, one should rather live possessed of inner renunciation.
That is the highest knowledge.

Therefore, forgetting your personality,
try to realize your identity with God.

Knowledge

"Does a man of knowledge ever fear rebirth?"

Does a man of knowledge ever fear rebirth?
He does not commit any indiscretion.
It is the ignorant people who are always seized with fear.
They alone get entangled and become polluted by sin.

To question too much is not good.
It is difficult to properly assimilate even one thought.
Now why should you trouble your mind
by harboring ten thoughts.

Dive deep with the noble idea that you have received.
Repeat the holy name,
meditate upon it,
keep good company,
and subdue the ego by all means.

My child, read a small portion of the Gita daily
and also the Kathamrita of the Master
and Sri Ramakrishna Punthi.

Many other books about the Master have also been published.
Read them.
Do not indulge in dry reasoning, though,
but rather acquire intense devotion.

Even the wise can hardly realize
the nature of Brahman by argument.
Are Brahman and the Divine Mother objects of discussion?

DIVINE MOTHER AND HER POWER

"Mother
— in the end my Mother pervades
the whole universe."

After nondual knowledge dawns,
God and all else vanish into nothing.
Mother — in the end my Mother pervades the whole universe.
Everything becomes one.
This is the simple truth.

In the course of time
one does not even feel the existence of God.
After attaining true wisdom
one sees that gods and deities are all Maya.

Everything comes into existence in time and disappears in time.
Kali, the Mother of the Universe, is the Mother of all.
It is She alone that has begotten both good and evil.
Everything has come out of Her womb.

The Kundalini will awake.
Repetition of His name will lead to the goal.
Even if your mind does not become concentrated
you can repeat the holy name thousands of times.

One hears the Anahata-dhvani
prior to the arousing of the Kundalini.
But it is not possible without the grace of the Mother.

The holy sound comes from the right side.
Only when there is body consciousness does it come from the left.
Such things happen
when the power of the Kundalini becomes awakened.
The sound that comes from the right side is the real one.

In time, the mind itself becomes the Guru.
If one is able to pray to God
and meditate on Him for even two minutes with full concentration,
it is very good.

Listen, my child,
however spiritual a man may be,
he must pay the tax for the use of the body to the last farthing.

But the difference between a great soul
and an ordinary man is this:
The latter weeps while leaving the body,
whereas the former laughs.
Death seems to him a mere play.

How much of japa you do,
however much of work you perform, it is all for nothing.
If Mahamaya does not open the way,
is anything possible for one?

Oh bound soul!
Surrender, surrender!
Then alone will She take compassion on you
and leave your path open.

Affirmation

"Formerly one had to make many arrangements
to see the Holy Mother.
Now, sitting at one place, if someone applies one's heart,
one can duly find Her.
Discarding Her physical body,
the Mother is now bestowing Her blessings much more.
Whoever calls upon Her,
the indwelling Mother approaches them
and settles all their problems."